THE GIPSY VIOLIN

ALBUM OF
WORLD-FAMOUS GIPSY ROMANCES

ARRANGED FOR
VIOLIN AND PIANO

EDITED AND REVISED BY

W. RUSS-BOVELINO

✦

CONTENTS

1. TWO GUITARS, *Russian Air*
2. SLOWLY FLOWS THE RIVER MAROS (Maros vize), *Hungarian Gipsy Song*
3. DEEP SORROW, *Gipsy Air*
4. GOLDEN WHEAT (Ritka busa), *Czárdás*
5. THE SLEIGH RIDE (Repül a szan), *Hungarian Romance*
6. DON'T LEAVE ME (Nu m'abandona), *Gipsy Romance*
7. HUNGARIAN FANTASY by W. Russ-Bovelino
8. 100 KISSES I'LL STEAL FROM YOU (Tiz par czokot), *Hungarian Air*
9. BLACK EYES, *Russian Gipsy Romance*
10. RASPOSCHOL, *Russian Gipsy Air*
11. LAVOTTA, *Hungarian Serenade*
12. ONE KITTEN, TWO KITTENS (Egy cica, két cica), *Hungarian Song*
13. HEISSA TROIKA, *Russian Gipsy Waltz*
14. THE STARS IN THE SKY (Nincsen annyi tenger csillag), *Hungarian Gipsy Air*
15. WIND, TELL MY SWEETHEART (Suga a fülébe), *Gipsy Song*
16. GIPSY AIR by Kurt Steiner, arr. L. Kubanek
17. SINAI HORA, *Roumanian Dance*

✦

BOSWORTH
14 –15 Berners Street, London W1T 3LJ, UK
Exclusive Distributors: Music Sales Limited,
Newmarket Road, Bury St Edmunds, Suffolk IP33 3YB, UK

TWO GUITARS

Russian Song

Made in England
Imprimé en Angleterre
Tous droits d'exécution réservés
B. & Co. Ltd. 21368

SLOWLY FLOWS THE RIVER MAROS
(Maros vize)

Hungarian Gipsy Song

6

DEEP SORROW

Gipsy Air

GOLDEN WHEAT
(Ritka buza)

Czárdás

Rather fast

THE SLEIGH RIDE
(Repül a szan)

Hungarian Romance

Rather slowly

Somewhat faster

DON'T LEAVE ME
(Nu m'abandona)

Gipsy Romance

HUNGARIAN FANTASY

Wolfgang Russ-Bovelino

100 KISSES I'LL STEAL FROM YOU
(Tiz par csokot)

Hungarian Air

BLACK EYES

Russian Gipsy Romance

RASPOSCHOL

Russian Gipsy Air

LAVOTTA

Hungarian Serenade

Made in England
Imprimé en Angleterre

Tous droits d'exécution réservés

ONE KITTEN, TWO KITTENS

(Egy cica, két cica)

Hungarian Song

HEISSA TROIKA

Tempo di Valse

Russian Gipsy Waltz

THE STARS IN THE SKY
(Nincsen, annyi tenger csillag)

Hungarian Gipsy Air

WIND, TELL MY SWEETHEART
(Suga a fülébe)

Gipsy Song

GIPSY AIR

by Kurt Steiner, arr. L. Kubanek

Friss-Allegro

SINAI HORA

Roumanian Dance

Printed in England

Master Melodies from the Classics

Melodies Célèbres de Maîtres Classiques

Schöne Melodien Klassischer Meister

For Violin and Piano

Pour Violon et Piano

Für Violine und Klavier

In progressive order arranged by

Arrangées et classées progressivement par

Eingerichtet und fortschreitend geordnet von

Leopold J. Beer

Vol. I (I. Pos.)

	Viol.	Piano Pag.
Alt-Wiener Weise. Old Viennese Air. Vieil air viennois	4	8
Beethoven, Ich liebe dich. I love thee. Je t'aime	2	4
Couperin, Menuett. Minuet. Menuet	12	28
Couperin, Sœur Monique	6	12
Händel, Aria	11	26
Händel, Largo	11	24
Händel, Menuett aus Samson. Minuet from Samson. Menuet de Samson	7	14
Haydn, Menuett. Minuet. Menuet	13	29
Marpurg, Menuett. Minuet. Menuet	3	6
Martini, Gavotte	1	2
Schubert, Deutsche Tänze. German Dances. Danses allemandes	8	18
Schubert, Horch, horch. Hark! Hark! the Lark. Écoute, l'alouette	16	39
Schumann, An den Sonnenschein. O, Sunshine, O, Sunshine. Au soleil	5	10
Weber, Sonatine	14	33

Vol. II (I.—III. Pos.)

	Viol.	Piano Pag.
Beethoven, Menuett. Minuet. Menuet	10	24
Beethoven, Türkischer Marsch. Turkish March. Marche turque	11	27
Couperin, Sicilienne	4	10
Dussek, Rondo	9	21
Händel, Air	13	32
Händel, Menuett. Minuet. Menuet	1	3
Händel, Sarabande	8	20
Liszt, Consolation No. 4	14	33
Marcello, Largo	15	36
Mozart, Allegro	3	7
Mozart, Menuett	2	4
Oginsky, Polonaise No. 2	16	38
Schumann, Träumerei. Dreaming. Rêverie	12	30
Schumann, Von fremden Menschen und Ländern. Foreign Lands and People. Des Pays lointains	12	31
Weber, Rondo	5	12

Vol. III (I.—V. Pos.)

	Viol.	Piano Pag.
Beethoven, Adagio aus Pathétique. Adagio from Pathétique. Adagio de la pathétique	1	2
Chopin, Op. 40 No. 1. Polonaise	4	10
Haydn, Ochsenmenuett. Ox's Minuet. Menuet de bœuf	3	8
Leclair, Sarabande et Tambourin	10	31
Liszt, Liebesträume No. 3. Rêves d'amour (Nocturne) No. 3	6	18
Schubert, Op. 94 No. 6. Moment Musical	7	24
Wagner, Preislied. Prize Song. Chant de concours	8	27
Wagner, Träume. Dreams. Rêves	12	36
Zipoli, Aria	2	6

BOSWORTH & CO. LTD.